I Apologize
for the Eyes
in My Head

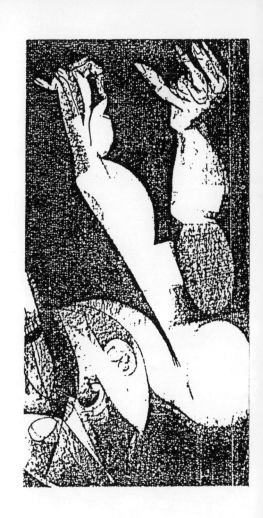

I Apologize for the Eyes in My Head

Yusef Komunyakaa

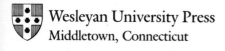 Wesleyan University Press
Middletown, Connecticut

Some of these poems first appeared in these anthologies and periodicals: *Black American Literature Forum, The Black Warrior Review, Callaloo, Cincinnati Poetry Review, Colorado State Review, Durak, Hambone, Ironwood, Kayak, MSS, New Orleans Review, The North American Review, Open Places, The Penny Dreadful, Ploughshares, Poetry Now, Pulpsmith, The Reaper, River Styx, Shankpainter, TBR, Tendril,* and *Writers Forum.*

"The Vicious," of "The Beast & the Burden," page 67, appeared in *Copacetic,* copyright © 1984 by Yusef Komunyakaa.

I wish to thank the Fine Arts Work Center at Provincetown and the National Endowment for the Arts for fellowships that enabled me to complete this book. YK

This book is supported by a grant from the National Endowment for the Arts.

The illustration facing the title page is based on a painting by Harold Rubin.

All inquiries and permissions requests should be addressed to the Publisher, Wesleyan University Press, 110 Mt. Vernon Street, Middletown, Connecticut 06457.

Distributed by Harper & Row Publishers, Keystone Industrial Park, Scranton, Pennsylvania 18512.

LIBRARY OF CONGRESS CATALOGING IN PUBLICATION DATA

Komunyakaa, Yusef.
   I apologize for the eyes in my head.

   (Wesleyan poetry)
   I. Title. II. Series.
PS3561.O45512 1986   811'.54   85-10504
ISBN 0-8195-5144-9 (alk. paper)
ISBN 0-8195-6148-7 (pbk. : alk. paper)

Manufactured in the United States of America

FIRST EDITION
WESLEYAN POETRY

for Mandy Jane Sayer, a natural-born seer

Contents

I

It is not merely with his whole soul, it is with his entire being that the poet approaches the poem. What presides over the poem is not the most lucid intelligence, or the most acute sensibility, but an entire experience: all the women loved, all the desires experienced, all the dreams dreamed, all the images received or grasped, the whole weight of the body, the whole weight of the mind. All lived experience. All the possibility.

—Aimé Césaire, *Poetry and Knowledge,*
translated from the French by A. James Arnold

Unnatural State of
the Unicorn

Introduce me first as a man.
Don't mention superficial laurels
the dead heap up on the living.
I am a man. Cut me & I bleed.
Before embossed limited editions,
before fat artichoke hearts marinated
in rich sauce & served with imported wines,
before antics & Agnus Dei,
before the stars in your eyes
mean birth sign or Impression,
I am a man. I've scuffled
in mudholes, broken teeth in a grinning skull
like the moon behind bars. I've done it all
to be known as myself. No titles.
I have principles. I won't speak
on the natural state of the unicorn
in literature or self-analysis.
I have no birthright to prove,
no insignia, no secret
password, no fleur-de-lis.
My initials aren't on a branding iron.
I'm standing here in unpolished
shoes & faded jeans, sweating
my manly sweat. Inside my skin,
loving you, I am this space
my body believes in.

Lightshow

Lightning dances down a naked
wire, while I sit at a window
reading my cards. The High Priestess
says I'm wrong about losses.
What would change this story,
an overnight ice age,
a telephone call to say
love's over?
Watching August's lightshow
shimmy up & down barred windows,
butterflies grow in my belly.
Some fear close to the bone ignites
the brain stem like a black wick.
Each day I badger myself with harder questions,
knowing how paper draws lightning.
Hologrammed gods pop neon whips,
cries leap out of the wood,
& the cards go momentarily indigo
in my hands. Answers elude,
fire runs under the skin,
thunder rolls out to a blue precipice
like artillery rounds—
pieces of afternoon torn off,
as if the brain's collapsed.
I feel like a devil's decoy
at this window, but I can't move
till The Hanged Man says *yes*.

Sorrow

She's on Main Street
lifting her yellow skirt.
Her perfume's a strange lucidity
or, more exactly, a pestilence.
She calls me her sweetheart,
her unlucky boy, her favorite ghost
in the looking glass.
                    Suddenly
she has her tongue in my mouth.
I brace myself against her;
already bigger than life,
she puts her head together with God's
until her call sign breaks in
& sends fighters into the sky.

Gazing through grey wood slats
of the poorhouse, I see her in a valley
ablaze with hyacinth & atropine.
In a Paris café, self-exiled,
I glimpse her sipping espresso,
eyeing the front door,
leafing through a copy of *The Tale
of the Devil's Fart*.
                  I spot her again
in Rio playing a concertina
in a roadhouse. Just as I step off
a curb in Mission Viejo
I notice her in a red sports car,
gunning the engine. At midnight
she climbs into bed, smiling,
her weight no more than a clue.
The bedsprings begin a low moan.

Touch-up Man

I playact the three monkeys
carved over the lintel of a Japanese shrine,
mouthing my mantra: *I do
what I'm told.* I work
from Mr. Pain's notecards;
he plants the germ of each idea.
And I'm careful not to look
at his private secretary's legs,
as I turn the harvest through the dumb-mill
of my hands. Half-drunk
with my tray of bright tools,
I lean over the enlarger,
in the light table's chromatic glare
where I'm king, doctoring photographs,
airbrushing away the corpses.

How I See Things

I hear you were
sprawled on the cover of *Newsweek*
with freedom marchers, those years
when blood tinted the photographs,
when fire leaped into the trees.

Negatives of nightriders
develop in the brain.
The Strawberry Festival Queen
waves her silk handkerchief,
executing a fancy high kick

flashback through the heart.
Pickups with plastic Jesuses
on dashboards head for hoedowns.
Men run twelve miles into wet cypress
swinging bellropes. Ignis fatuus can't be blamed

for the charred Johnson grass.
Have we earned the right
to forget, forgive
ropes for holding
to moonstruck branches?

Every last stolen whisper
the hoot owl echoes
turns leaves scarlet.
Hush shakes the monkeypod
till pink petal-tongues fall.

You're home in New York.
I'm back here in Bogalusa
with one foot in pinewoods.
The mockingbird's blue note
sounds to me like *please,*

please. A beaten song
threaded through the skull
by cross hairs.
Black hands still turn blood red
working the strawberry fields.

Insufficient Blue

At St. Marks Bookshop I buy
Berrigan's *So Going Around Cities,*
saying, "I have to meet him
someday." July 4th's
fireworks boom away dusk.

Out on the street starclusters
rainbow & bottle rockets
arc across New York.
Summer hangs up a scarlet cape,
what's left unsaid between lovers.

Something happened in another city
& we're here to patch things up.
Forget. Forgive. Stop
reading between lines, thumbing
snowy pages from a woeful season.

Lately love's shown us
such ugly scars,
such criminal sweetness.
Strings of firecrackers pop
& spook dogs down the street.

At the Centre Pub I'm hungry
for a hamburger & you want onion soup.
The wine's magical. A woman at the table
across from us sits careless as a lie.
Her dress is dreamy blue
& she's wearing no underwear.

How could we have known
Ted Berrigan was somewhere
baffling the Angel of Death?
Even though night's crimson stars
kept raining down on us.

The Thorn Merchant

There are teeth marks
on everything he loves.
When he enters the long room
more solemn than a threadbare Joseph coat,
the Minister of Hard Knocks & Golden Keys
begins to shuffle his feet.
The ink on contracts disappears.
Another stool pigeon leans
over a wrought-iron balcony.
Blood money's at work.
While men in black wetsuits
drag Blue Lake, his hands dally
at the hem of his daughter's skirt.

In the brain's shooting gallery
he goes down real slow.
His heart suspended in a mirror,
shadow of a crow over a lake.
With his fingers around his throat
he moans like a statue
of straw on a hillside.
Ready to auction off his hands
to the highest bidder,
he knows how death waits
in us like a light switch.

The Thorn Merchant's
Right-Hand Man

Well, that's Pretty Boy Emeritus
alias Leo the Machine, great-grandson
of Eddie the Immune, a real ladies' man
in his handmade elevated Spanish shoes.
It's funny how he walks into town
with just a bouquet or violin
& lost faces reappear, eclipsed
by fedoras in bulletproof
limousines. A looted brain case
succumbs & a cage of prayers
sways in night air. Pretty Boy throws a kiss
to death, a paradoxical star in each eye. Naturally
he's surprised when he stumbles
& snags his suit coat on an ice pick.
It had to happen. He's caught
in a Texaco john humming the Mass in D.
The fight moves out to the corner
of Midsummer Avenue & Galante Blvd.
like two men tussling with red lanterns.
Pretty Boy's shoelaces tied together,
the full moon behind flowering manzanita
deserts him with his tongue in pawn
clear down to where a plea forms
the root word for flesh.

After the Heart's Interrogation

In December's slaughterhouse
I'm still standing my ground.
The wall clock picks itself apart.
What's left of my life stumbles forward
in heavy boots. The trouble is,
I know what it all means.

There's more to come. A white goat
is staring into windows again.
Bats clog the chimney like rags.
An angel in the attic
mends a torn wing. Dog-eared luck.
The gun cocking outside
my front door is another question
I'm here to answer.

Happy-Go-Lucky's
Wolf Skull Dream Mask

OK, lift this mask
up to your eyes, over your face,
a perfect fit.

Well, Mr. Magnifico,
what do you see? How's your world?

Now you must live on silence.
I know you can only see gold
glistening with another's sweat,
hear only a strand of barbed wire
a half-mile in the heart, music

of poison sumac.
In your well-earned lunacy
you can smell death coming.
There's something you just can't
shake; you bite into it—
laced up through eyeholes of self-pity.

I know there's a blank space
big enough for a man to shove his fist into,
where your heart used to be
playing its black keys.

The Heart's Graveyard Shift

I lose faith in my left hand
not because my dog Echo's eloped
with ignis fatuus into pinewoods
or that my limp's unhealed
after 13 years. What can go wrong
goes wrong, & between loves an empty
space defines itself like a stone's weight
helps it to sink into earth.
My devil-may-care attitude
returns overnight, the bagwoman
outside the 42nd Street Automat
is now my muse. I should know
by heart the schema, routes
A & B, points where we
flip coins, heads or tails,
to stay alive. Between loves
I crave danger; the assassin's cross hairs
underline my point of view.

                         Between loves,
with a pinch of madness tucked under
the tongue, a man might fly off the handle
& kill his best friend over a penny.
His voice can break into butterflies
just as the eight ball cracks
across deep-green felt,
growing silent with something unsaid
like a mouth stuffed with nails.
He can go off his rocker, sell the family
business for a dollar, next morning
pull a Brink's job & hijack a 747.
He can hook up with a woman in silver
spike heels who carries a metallic blue guitar
or he can get right with Jesus
through phenobarbital.

                        Between loves
I sing all night with the jukebox:
"Every man's gotta cry for himself."
I play chicken with the Midnight Special
rounding Dead Man's Curve, enthralled
by the northern lights & machinery
of falling stars. Internal solstice,
my body, a poorly rigged by-pass
along Desperado Ave., taking me away
from myself. Equilibrium's whorehouses.
Arcades scattered along the eastern seaboard.
I search dead-colored shells for clues,
visions, for a thread of meat,
untelling interior landscapes.
A scarecrow dances away with my shadow.
Between loves I could stand all day
at a window watching honeysuckle open
as I make love to the ghosts
smuggled inside my head.

Hard Up

The quiet way the sun hangs dead center
of everything, I'm looking through a woman's dress.
Her name might be Beatrice.
Noon trees, appendages of light, nothing to do
    with love.
Yes, we're falling over our two shoes
to escape each other.
My soul comes toward her, a shaking calabash sonata.
Today's naked. She runs under a pink umbrella.
I run under a locust tree. She runs behind a billboard
proclaiming: BETTER BUY STOCK IN BOMB SHELTERS.
I run into a telephone booth.
I dial my mother's number.
I come at her two directions at once,
skirting the edge of nowhere to run now.
She smiles, gives in, hopelessly
trying to hide under her light blue dress.

Boy Wearing
a Dead Man's Clothes

1

I must say I never liked
gabardine's wornout shine.

Cold weather fills this coat,
& the shoulders have drooped anyhow!

Jesus, his yellow silk handkerchief;
I'm keeping this next to my heart.

The police chief's daughter's smile
has started to peel off

the curled photo I found
here in his breast pocket.

2

Blue denim cap, no other
crown for a poor man's head.

I wear it the same angle
he did, hipper than thou.

If I tilt it over my eyes,
a bit to the left this way,

cut the sky in half,
can I see the world

through his eyes? Cloud-cap
washed till there's hardly any blue left.

3

Uncle Jimmy's flowered shirt
keeps its shape. Body's character—

enamored of sweat, touch
gone out of the cloth,

no dark red map widening
across my chest to recall

that night.
Sleeves filled with silence.

The lipstick won't
come off.

4

I don't belong here. I
can't help but say

to Uncle's cordovan boots,
Get me outta East Texas, back to L.A.,

but please don't take me
by their place: Four weeks ago, that time

I saw him & Mrs. Overstreet
kissing in the doorway,

& Mr. Overstreet drunk
with his head on the table.

Gift Horse

Your wife's forty-five
today & you've promised her
someone like me, did I
hear you right? You
wave a hundred-dollar bill
under my nose & a diamond
of snowlight falls through
the bar's isinglass walls
as Dylan comes up on the jukebox.

You saw me hustling pool tables
for nickels & dimes, now my refusal
rocks you like a rabbit punch
in the solar plexus. You pull
snapshots from your wallet.
Yeah, she does look like
Shirley Jones in *Elmer Gantry*.
You say you're a man
who loves the truth.
And maybe my mistake is
I believe you.

I know the dark oath
flesh makes with earth.
You drive a hard bargain
for a stone to rest your head on.
On the jukebox, Otis Redding's "Dock of the Bay."
Days fall around us
bigger than the snowstorm
that drove you in here
to dodge wind driving pine needles
through the hearts of birds.

You up the ante another fifty.
My bottle of beer sweats
a cool skin for us both.
You blow smoke-ring halos
for dust-colored angels among tinsel,
reindeer & year-round Christmas lights,
where sexual hunger's like ripe apples,
but by now you must know I can't
sleep in your bed while you drive
around the countryside till

sunrise, taking the blind
curves on two wheels.

The Music That Hurts

Put away those insipid spoons.
The frontal lobe horn section went home hours ago.
The trap drum has been kicked
down the fire escape,
& the tenor's ballad amputated.
Inspiration packed her bags.
Her caftan recurs in the foggy doorway
like brain damage; the soft piano solo of her walk
evaporates; memory loses her exquisite tongue,
looking for "green silk stockings with gold seams"
on a nail over the bathroom mirror.
Tonight I sleep with Silence,
my impossible white wife.

When in Rome
—Apologia

Please forgive me, sir,
for getting involved

in the music—
it's my innate weakness

for the cello: so human.
Please forgive me
for the attention

I've given your wife
tonight, sir.

I was taken in by her
strand of pearls,
enchanted by a piano
riff in the cortex,
by a secret

anticipation. I don't know
what came over me, sir.

After three Jack Daniel's
you must overlook
my candor, my lack of
sequitur.

I could talk
about Odysseus

& Athena, sexual
flowers, autogamy
or Nothingness.

I got carried away
by the swing of her hips.

But take no offense
if I return to the matter

as if hormonal.
I must confess
my love for black silk, sir.
I apologize for
the eyes in my head.

The Thorn Merchant's Wife

She meditates on how rocks rise
in Bluebird Canyon, how hills
tremble as she makes love
to herself, how memories drift
& nod like belladonna
kissing the ground.

She remembers the first time, there
in his flashy two-tone Buick.
That night she was a big smile
in the moon's broken-down alley.
When she became the Madonna of Closed Eyes
nightmares bandaged each other
with old alibis & surgical gauze,
that red dress he fell for
turned to ghost cloth
in some bagwoman's wardrobe.

She thinks about the gardener's son.
But those black-haired hours only lasted
till the shake dancer's daughter
got into his blood & he grew sober—
before solitaire began to steal
her nights, stringing an opus
of worry beads, before Morphine
leaned into the gold frame.

The Thorn Merchant's Mistress

I was on my high
horse then. I
wore red with ease

& I knew how
to walk. There
were men undressing me

everywhere I went,
& women wishing
themselves in my place,

a swan unfractured
by August. I was still
a girl. If they

wanted culture,
I said Vivaldi
& Plato's Cave.

If they wanted
the streets, I said
Fuck you.

I knew how
to plead, Wait, Wait,
till I caught the eye

of some *deus ex
machina*. I was in
a deep dance

pulling the hidden
strings of nude
shadows. But when his car
drove by so slow
my heart caught
like a fat moth

in spider web. Goddamn!
I didn't know
how to say No.

Somewhere Else

Making angels in the snow.
We aren't ourselves, hardly
trusting what we've become.
The years now weigh
as much as the bad king's crown.
I find it harder to dance,
shy father of my own
downfall, no more than water
singing through the drainpipe
at a black speed.
A man in another season
laughs beside a woman
& they're the only song
in Manitou Springs' night air.
Loss, what's that? Those two
hands which once held mine
now holding up a blanket
of snow—does this qualify?
Frankly, all I can say is
I've been to a funny place
inside myself, where simple
answers fall like ashes
through an iron grate.

After Summer
Fell Apart

I can't touch you.
His face always returns;
we exchange long looks
in each bad dream
& what I see, my God.
Honey, sweetheart,
I hold you against me
but nothing works.
Two boats moored,
rocking between nowhere
& nowhere.
A bone inside me whispers
maybe tonight,
but I keep thinking
about the two men wrestling nude
in Lawrence's *Women in Love.*
I can't get past
reels of breath unwinding.
He has you. Now
he doesn't. He has you
again. Now he doesn't.

You're at the edge of azaleas
shaken loose by a word.
I see your rose-colored
skirt unfurl.
He has a knife
to your throat,
night birds come back
to their branches.

A hard wind raps at the door,
the new year prowling
in a black overcoat.
It's been six months
since we made love.
Tonight I look at you
hugging the pillow,
half smiling in your sleep.
I want to shake you & ask
who. Again I touch myself,
unashamed, until
his face comes into focus.
He's stolen something
from me & I don't know
if it has a name or not—
like counting your ribs
with one foolish hand
& mine with the other.

Uncertainty in Blue

for Carolyne

I'd feel lost as Lorca
here in the Big Apple
if we weren't holding hands.
Years run together, days drop
off the blue edge. Faces
dissolve into a blameless mist.

In Washington Square
I notice body language,
who's leaning towards whom.
Black hands on a weary clock.
Across morning two crooked
trees grow out of each other,

married to a blue background.
We watch skaters daredevil,
weave silver circumferences
& play loop-the-loop,
barely escaping head-on collisions
with totems in bloom.

Plugged into their boogie boxes,
they don't see July.
New Wave & Punk Rock
jolt the Modern Jazz Quartet
in our heads from the night before
at Carnegie Hall. We know a hard light

forces the pale bud to red,
but we're surprised to learn
what's unsaid. We bend rules & sidestep.
When we find ourselves arguing about Picasso's
African masks I laugh, knowing
we sometimes give so we can take.

The Brain to the Heart

Stars tied to breath
don't have to be there
when you look.
No more than drops
of blood on ginkgo
leaves & inconsequential

eggs & frog spittle
clinging to damp grass.
Sure, I've seen doubts
clustered like peacock
eyes flash green fire.
So what?

When days are strung together,
the hourglass fills
with worm's dirt.
What do you take
the brain for? I know
how hard you work

in that dark place, but
I can't be tied down
to shadows of men
in trenches you won't
forget. You look at
a mulberry leaf

like a silkworm does, with all your insides,
but please don't ask me to be responsible.

Audacity of the Lower Gods

I know salt marshes that move along like one big
trembling wing. I've noticed insects
shiny as gold in a blues singer's teeth
& more keenly calibrated than a railroad watch,
but at heart I'm another breed.

The audacity of the lower gods—
whatever we name we own.
Diversiloba, we say, unfolding poison oak.
Lovers go untouched as we lean from bay windows
with telescopes trained on a yellow sky.

I'd rather let the flowers
keep doing what they do best.
Unblessing each petal,
letting go a year's worth of white
death notes, busily unnaming themselves.

The Falling-Down Song

Here I am
with one foot on a floating platform
        breaking myself into small defeats—
I'm the ghost of a moneychanger
        & halo of flies, half-moon of false teeth
unable to bite bread. Please
go, & tell no one you've seen me under the cypress,
        a fool-hearted footstool,
                termites in my two
                        sad wooden
                            legs,
sawdust in my black leather shoes.

Syzygy

Darling, I understand
this is the Year of the Dog,
so please be careful.
Walk only those well-lit streets
& know who your friends are.
We can all take the Fifth.
Or, better yet, play crazy.
Can move into the Rockies & make love
to mountain sheep in springtime,
listening to white rivers sing
through our broken hearts.
We can fool ourselves
with a touch of lust
under our tongues. Indifference
would be a better word.
We can always kill
some integral part of ourselves,
let the right hand hold
down the left,
crying in our sleep
OK, you bastards
come & get me, if you're bad.
Manifestoes to green frogs
on lily pads. Across
the estuary where dogbane
blooms under the Dog Star,
birds have a song called Death
in their throats. We
put our eyeteeth in hock,
& swear we didn't
hear a thing.

The Thorn Merchant's Son

Using an old water-stained
Seven Year Itch movie poster
as his dartboard, he places
all six into the bull's-eye.
The phonograph clicks silently,
playing "Teen Angel" the tenth time.
Sipping a Pepsi-Cola,
he moves over to *Pretty Baby*
unrolled on his daddy's desk.
He runs his tongue around
the edge of her smile,
then picks up a paperweight
& shakes it till the black horse
disappears inside the glass.
Grey-eyed opacity, low cloud
coming over the room, he throws
a wooden puzzle against a wall
& the fist-shaped piece
flies apart like a clay pigeon.
He stares fifteen minutes
at a tintype face
so blue it's hardly there.
With a little dance step
he eases over & props an elbow
on the window sill, aiming
his high-powered binoculars
at a woman's bedroom window.

I Apologize

My mind wasn't even there.
Mirage, sir. I didn't see
what I thought I saw.
Que será, será. That's that.
I was in my woman's bedroom
removing her red shoes & dress.
I'm just like the rest of the world:
No comment; no way, Jose;
I want spring always
dancing with the pepper trees.
I was miles away, I saw nothing!
Did I say their diamond rings
blinded me & I nearly lost my head?
I think it was how the North
Star fell through plate glass.
I don't remember what they wore.
What if I said they were
only shadows of overcoats
stooped in the doorway
where the light's bad?
No, no one roughed me up last night.
Sir, there's no story to change.
I heard no names. There were no
distinguishing marks or other clues.
No slip of the tongue. This morning
I can't even remember who I am.

1984

The year burns an icon
into the blood. Birdlime
discolors the glass domes
& roof beams grow shaky as old men
in the lobby of Heartbreak Hotel.
Purple oxide gas lamps light
the way out of this paradise.
We laugh behind masks & lip-sync Cobol.
We're transmitters for pigeons
with microphones in their heads.
Yellow sky over stockyards,
& by the grace of God
rockets hum in white silos
buried in Kansas wheat fields
or nailed to some ragged hill
zoned as a perfect fearscape.

We say, "I've seen it all."
Bombardment & psychic flux,
not just art nouveau tabula rasa
or double helix. We're ancient mariners
counting wishbones, in supersonic hulls
humming the falconer's ditty
over a banged-up job.
Three Mile Island blooms
her dreamworld as we wait
on the edge of our chairs
for the drunk radiologist.
Such a lovely view—
Big Brother to shadows
slipping under the door
where the millstones are stored.

We sing the ghost-catcher's madrigal.
The end of what? To count dismembered years
we say Gandhi, JFK, King,
leafing through names & faces. Waves
of locusts fall like black snow
in our sleep. Grackles
foresee ruins & battlements
where the Bone Breakers & God Squad
have had a good old time—
destined to sleep under
swaying trestles, as yes-men
crowded into a bad season,
listening all night to a calliope
hoot the equinox.

Since our hair's standing up
on the backs of our necks,
we must be on to something good,
Oppenheimer, right? Killjoy's
perched like Khan of the Golden Horde
on the back of a prisoner,
& we sit eating crow,
picking teeth with gold toothpicks.
Angels playing with trick mirrors,
sweet on a Minotaur in the dark
muscular air of a penny arcade.
We can transplant broken hearts
but can we put goodness back into them?

Brass knuckles flash
& this year is like flesh
torn under a lover's eye.
The end of what?
Going after posthumous love letters
dumped in black holes
light-years away, we line up
for practice runs with portable
neutron bombs strapped
to our backs—lopsided fun houses
where everyone wants to be
king of the stacked deck.

Streamlined androids construct
replicas three thousand miles away.
We guardians of uglier things to come
with our camera obscuras,
light vigil candles
& work the White Angel
bread line. Following the lunar crab
& loving the skyline, we discover
there's nothing to hold down tombstones,
lovers wishing upon astronauts
flashier than rock stars.

Alloyed against common sense,
somehow we're all King Lears
calling forth kingdom come—
scherzo for brimstone.
Fireworks bring in the New Year
& Zeus the confused robot
punches a fist through a skylight
as he dances across the floor
with his mechanical bride
doing a bionic two-step.

Hammered silver,
those badges we wear:
U-235 UTOPIA.
Made in America.
"Give us enough time,
we'll make the damn thing.
Let's look at the manual.
OK, here's *human breath*
on page 319."

Weather wars hang in skies
over the Third World. The dead
keep walking toward the sea
with everything they own
on their backs. Caught off guard
our falsehoods break into parts
of speech, like mayflies
on windshields of white Corvettes.

We're stargazers, weirdos,
prestidigitators in bluesy
bedrooms, on private trips
to the moon. The end of what?
We lock our hearts
into idle, not sure
of this world or the next.

Let's come down to earth.
Let's forget those video wrist watches
& "E.T." dolls triggered
by interstellar sundials
where electric eyes
hum on 18-carat key chains

& Dr. Strangelove tracks
the titanium gods. Let's go
beyond Devil's Triangle,
back to where the heart knows.
All the machines are on.

We sleepwalk among black roses
like characters in a dime novel,
& psychotherapy
can't erase the sign of the beast.

Dreambook Bestiary

Fear's Understudy

Like some lost part of a model kit
for Sir Dogma's cracked armor
an armadillo merges with night.
It rests against a mossy stone.
A steel-gray safe-deposit box,
ground level, two quicksilver eyes
peer out from under a coral helmet
color of fossil. It lives
encased in an asbestos hull
at the edge of a kingdom
of blackberries in quagmire,
in a grassy daydream,
sucked into its shield
by logic of flesh.

The Art of Atrophy

The possum plays dead
as Spanish moss, a seasoned actor
giving us his dumb show.
He dreams of ripe persimmons,
watching a dried stick
beside a white thunderstone,
with one eye half-open, a grin
slipping from the crooked corners
of his mouth, that old silver moon
playing tricks again. How long
can he play this waiting game,
till the season collapses,
till blowflies, worms, & ants
crawl into his dull coat
& sneak him away under

the evening star? Now
he's a master escape artist
like Lazarus, the gray
lining from a workman's glove
lost in frost-colored leaves.

Heart of the Rose Garden
A cluster of microscopic mouths
all working at once—

ants improve the soil, sift dust
through a millennium of wings.

They subsist on fear, drawn
to the lovebone,

to the base of the skull
where a slow undermining takes shape.

Under moonlight they begin their
instinctual autopsy, sensing

when grief tracks
someone down in her red patent-leather shoes,

when a man's soul
slips behind a headstone.

Glimpse
Near a spidery cage of grass
this cripple inches sideways up a sandy trail
with its little confiscated burden.
Just bigger than a man's thumbnail,
light as the shadow of a bone.

The sea falls short again. Claws unfold.
Its body almost creeps out. Morning
ticks away. Playing yes, no,
maybe so, it places its dome-shack
down on the sand & backs off,
surveying for the first tremor of loss.

Underside of Light

Centipede. Tubular, bright egg sac
trailing like a lodestone (unable to say
which is dragging which) out of damp compost:
biological soil, miasma, where lightning
starts like a sharp pain in god's spine.

In its armor, this sentinel rises
from a vault of double blackness.
This vegetal love forecasting April
crawls toward murdering light,
first thing tied to last.

Two Cranial Murals

She's at the mouth of a river
singing tongueless mantras
among reeds. A green parrot
picks up a birth cry
from cattails & broken grass.
No word yet for flesh.
If the gods have mouths now,
they say *raven, raven.*
Darkness wound in camphor
trees, the first smile
unconscious as a mooncalf's
under the sky's white belly—
the first eclipse of mind & body.
She winds the blood's clock.

Happy?
Who knows.
The tree gods
test a flowering branch over the river:
Sway-jig, sway-jig, sway-jig.
They ease out to its white verge—
half in this world, half in another,
ugly & beautiful. Caressing sky,
he reaches for a black-
orange butterfly on her head.
They linger there, caught up
in the slow blue song.
Then they invent a game
called Push & Shove.

Jonestown: More Eyes
for *Jadwiga's Dream*

After Rousseau

Brighter than crisp new money.
Birds unfold wings into nervous fans,
adrift like breath-drawn kites, among
tremulous fronds with flowers crimson
as muzzle flash. Tropic silk, root color,
ocean green, they float to tree limbs
like weary scarves.

Hidden eyes deepen the memory
between sunrise & nightmare. Pine-box builders
grin with the pale soothsayer presiding over
this end of songs. The day's a thick hive
of foliage, not the moss grief deposits
on damp stones—we're unable to tell where
fiction bleeds into the real.

Some unspoken voice, small as a lizard's,
is trying to obey the trees.
Green birds flare up behind church bells
against the heartscape: if only
they'd fold their crepe-paper wings
over bruised eyes & see nothing
but night in their brains.

Landscape for
the Disappeared

Lo & behold. Yes, peat bogs
in Louisiana. The dead
stumble home like swamp fog,
our lost uncles & granddaddies
come back to us almost healed.
Knob-fingered & splayfooted,
all the has-been men
& women rise through nighttime
into our slow useless days.

Live oak & cypress
counting these shapes in a dance
human forms aren't made for. Faces
waterlogged into their own
pure expression, unanswerable
questions on their lips.

Dumbstruck premonitions rise
from the heckle-grass
to search us out.
Guilty, sings the screech owl.
I hear the hair keeps growing
in the grave. Here
moss lets down a damp light.

We call back the ones
we've never known, with stories
more ours than theirs.
The wind's low cry
their language, a lunar rainbow
lost among Venus's-flytraps
yellowing in frog spittle & downward mire,
boatloads of contraband
guns & slot machines dumped
through the years.

Here's this lovely face so black
with marsh salt. Her smile,
a place where minnows swim.
All the full presence
shiny as a skull under the skin.
Say it again—we are
spared nothing.

Articulation
& Class

The hangman points out
   to the condemned man
      a purple martin

swooping up a jade-green dragonfly,
   then drops the black hood
      over his head.

In the Labor Camp
of Good Intentions

There's an angel
snapping his fingers.
He stands nonchalantly outside his low
guardshack made from astral dogwood
braced by a Judas tree,
lifting his arms like torn
signal flags dissecting
the night, the shadow of a Doberman
rearing against its choke chain.
Like a man fanning flies, he just waves
the tooth-&-nail brigade through.
Possibly he does it to soothe
the blind itch under his tongue.

Good Joe

We prop him up
in his easy chair.
We give him a crew cut.
We dust off his blue serge.
We sing his favorite
golden oldies: "Dixie"
& "Ta-ra-ra-boom-de-ay!"
We clamp on his false
finger bones. We lead him
across the floor
saying, "Walk, walk."
We move in circles
dancing the McCarthy—
someone leans over & clicks in
his glass eye. All his ideas
come into focus;
we hear rats in the walls
multiplying.

Professors, photojournalists,
scholars of ashes in urns
buried a thousand years
off the Gulf of Mexico
sign loyalty oaths; actors
forget their meaty lines.
We shine his wing-tip Bostonians.
We bring him oyster stew,
bottles of Chivas Regal
on a jade serving tray.

We show him snapshots of lovers.
We give him a book of names,
turning the pages for him.
Some of us volunteer
to enter a room
where machines take each other apart
& put themselves back
together. We form
a line which spills out
the door, around the corner
for a whole city block,
& with bowed heads
pay protection.

Making Out with the
Dream-Shredding Machine

He throws his arms around
a wheel, hunches closer,
resting his head against
the bullheaded millstone
shiny as a shark's back.
Quasimodo taken in by
unmerciful smoothness,
while boldface roman letters
fall into his mouth like grain.
He poses in the broken angle
at which all angels come into
this world, gazing sideways
for a skylight,
pinned down in a full nelson
like Houdini on the floor
kissing his shadow good-bye.

In the Background of Silence

First, worms begin with a man's mind.
Then they eat away his left shoe
to answer his final question.
His heart turns into a gold thimble of ashes,
his bones remind bees of honeycomb,
he falls back into himself like dirt into a hole,
his soul fits into a matchbox
in the shirt pocket
of his brother's well-tailored uniform.

Not even a stray dog dares to stir in the plaza,
after the muzzle flash,
after black coffee & Benzedrine,
after the sign of the cross a hundred times,
after sorrow's skirt drops to the floor,
after the soldier pulls off his spit-shined boots
& crawls into bed with the prettiest woman in town.

Cinderella at Big Sur

His kisses airbrush over her
in shadow play. She lies there
clothed only with his naked
thoughts, feeling night's thistle-star
etch salt into her. "Good girl,"
says Midas, her benefactor.

There must be something she can believe in.
The Invisible Angel
wearing a gold silk dress.
The falsebottom of her nights
means she's in her own world;

not exactly under the influence,
whole in her habit of pure seeing—
tender root holding on to earth
or the hand that uproots.
He hands her three masks
of a young Howard Hughes.

How did she get here, & who's this man?
She's watched the hammer
strike the nail but doesn't
know why each nail holds
his cruel funhouse together.

Days come & go like water
over stones. Cocaine's
lost its kick. She sleeps under Midas's
shiny dome, but the kingdom
of worms eats through to where
passionflowers bleed open.

Olympia

Someone in this room
would rather see a swan
fucking Leda. A monocle sways
on a gold chain; someone
in this place would rather
see Jacob with an angel
in a compromising position.
Her awkward left hand says
Iago's outside a hidden door
eavesdropping at a keyhole
Manet painted over; not stammel—
black healed the mistake.
She wears coquettish high heels
in bed, a flower in her hair
seductive as a magnolia.
And he's a stand-in Othello
in his androgynous robe,
with a night-colored cat
beside him named Cliché.

"Everybody's Reading Li Po"
Silkscreened on a Purple T-Shirt

Li Po who?
Says the shoeless
woman moving toward me with
her faded aura, angry
at no one in this world.

Li Po who?
Murmurs December,
speaking in tongues
like the girl in Jackson Square.
Sweet stench of onion
eats at me as the wind
discovers an old man
asleep under newspapers.
His dream a slow leaf
on black water.

Li Po who?
Says the boy junkie, Ricardo.
Tied to night's string,
he sways under neon
like a black girl with red hair
in the doorway of Lucky's.

Li Po who?
Says the prostitute
on Avenue Z.
Smelling loud as a bag
of lavender sachet
spilled on the sidewalk.
Blue-veined pallor,
she lifts her skirt to show
what a diamond-studded
garter looks like.

For the Walking Dead

Veronica passes her cape between breath
& death, rehearsing
the body's old rhyme.
With boyish soldiers on their way
to the front, she dances
the slowdrag in a bar called
Pylos. White phosphorus blooms
five miles away, burning sky
for a long moment, mortars
rock in iron shoes cradled
by earth, within earshot
of carbines stuttering through
elephant grass. Canisters lobbed
over night hills whine
like moonstruck dogs. After-
silence falls into the valley.

Tunes on the outdated jukebox
take her back to St. Louis,
back to where the color of her eyes
served as no one's balsam.
"Please," they whisper in her ear
as she counts the unreturned
faces, pale beads on an abacus.
Skin-colored dawn unravels
& a gun turret pivots on a hill.
Amputated ghosts on the walls—
she pulls them to her,
knowing the bruise beforehand.
She lets them work her into
the bar's darkest corner.
They hold her, a shield
against everything they know.

Too Pretty for
Serious Business

Moonlight on ante-bellum skin—
how he has her
laid out in his mind,
wanting her to say snapdragon
& belladonna. Not to use words like blood,
shit, tiger cages,
that she doesn't know the score
written on the forehead.
Wearing his Billy the Kid grin,
he feels like a pair of boots
with iron spurs. He says, "Honey,
I'm the curator of parchment
skullcaps & broken promises."
He wants her on her back
studying a butterfly's weight
on a tree & singing "Old Black Joe."
He blows on a camellia
to break it open,
gives her a bloodstone,
saying, "Here.
See how hard it is;
now aren't you lucky?"
She says, "Hell no!"
He leans on his rosewood desk,
mumbling something about snow
& amber on Goat Mountain.

Child's Play

Hair slicked back as if
he just eased up out of
womb-water, the young man
wears a fatigue jacket.
The shoulder patch says
Seven Steps to Hell.
Dancing with the machine,
he tries to coax Thundarr
up from the black box
deep in the belly of metal.
The Cosmic Death's-Head
wars with Captain Sky.
A woman in punk-rocker black
plays Asteroids, leaning
her shadow against his
on the bus-terminal wall.
His hands work with chrome,
rockets zoom across the screen
silent as a sperm count.
His knuckles grow white
gripping the knobs,
with his collar turned up
like John Travolta's.
He gazes down in the glass
aiming for a clean kill,
not nearly as dangerous
as he wants you to think.

Raw Data for an
Unfinished Questionnaire

Did they expect to find
good horse sense, God
shrunken in a Mason jar
stashed in a cardboard box
at their feet? With
Einstein's brain in Witchita,
did questions grow
like a Saturday night
rainstorm, shadow of wrens
darkening office windows?
Did they really hope for
invisible tripwires tied
to doubt as they unrolled
Dead Sea Scrolls on a stainless-
steel table under a galaxy
of hot lamps, a whole day
of stars in a white room?
Far from his birthplace,
was it easier to tear away
his last song, end the violin
sonata soft as beeswax
held together by remorse,
& forget those high-school girls
at the pier holding red roses
to their breasts? Forgotten
among rumpled gray newspapers
23 years, how long did he dream
Hiroshima's black rain,
& did they recognize love
hiding in the frontal lobe?

The Beast & Burden:
Seven Improvisations

I
The Vicious

Fear threads its song
through the bones.
Syringe, stylus,
or pearl-handled stiletto?
He's fallen in love
with the Spanish garrote;
trailing a blue feather over the beast's belly
on down between his toes.
Night-long laughter
leaks from under the sheet-metal door.

Blackout.

———

He sits under a floodlight
mumbling that a theory of ants
will finally deal with us,

& reading My Lord Rochester
to a golden sky over Johannesburg,
a stray dog beside him, Sirius
licking his combat boots.

2

The Decadent

Herr Scalawag, Esq.
dances the come-on
in Miss Misery's
spike heels.
He does a hellcat
high step stolen
from Josephine Baker,
holding a fake flower
like a flimsy excuse.
A paper rose, poppy
odor of luck
& lust. Look,
he's placed himself
upon the night's maddening wheel,
reduced from flesh
into the stuff
dreams are made of.

                Hum-job,
his smile working
like a time-released
Mickey Finn.

3

The Esoteric

Unable to move the muse with narcotic
sweet talk, he muscles in on someone's grief.

He's on the glassy edge
of his stepping stone, a ghost
puppet stealing light from the real
world. With a wild guess
for spine, a face half-finished
on the blind lithographer's desk.

Canticle, cleftsong & heartriff
stolen out of another's mouth,
effigy's prologue & bravado.
He fingers his heirloom
Bible with rows of exed out names
& dried roses between yellow pages,

searching for an idiom
based on the color of his eyes.

4

The Sanctimonious

She wakes to find herself washing
the beast's wounds.
The Woman at the Well
with bare feet in compost,
emissary to the broken. She leans

her body against this born loser,
her hip into his ungodly mercy,
her hair sways with his breathing,
her mind intent on an hourglass
on a stone shelf. Bronze green.

By now, as they rock
in each other's embrace
in the cold half-light,
she knows every doubtful wish
inside his housebroken head.

5
The Vindictive

Smiley, the jailer
hums the bowstring's litany.
His pale voice breaks
into a bittersweetness,
his face no more
than a half-page
profile from a wanted poster.
The iron door eases open.
Blameful mask, memory's
notorious white glove
unstitches the heartstring.
His leaden stare tabulates
the spinal column like a throw
of the dice. Satisfied
defeat has taken root,
he smiles down at the prisoner
on the cell floor, his touch
burning like candlelight & crab lice
through black hair. Wagner's
Ring of the Nibelung
plays on radio across the corridor
& the smell of mignonette
comes through the bars. He
tightens his mystical sleephold—
a carbuncle of joy
underneath his kiss.

6

Exorcism

The beast's charisma
unravels the way a smoke flower
turns into dust. Hugging
the shadow of a broken wing
beauty & ugliness conspire.
Forced to use his weight perfectly
against himself, the beast is
transmogrified into the burden
& locked in wooden stocks
braced by a cross to bear.
O how geranium-scented melancholia
works on the body—
smell of ether, gut string
trailing lost memories.
Detached from whatever remains,
one note of bliss still burns his tongue.

7

Epilogue: Communion

The beast & the burden lock-step waltz. Tiger lily &
screwworm, it all adds up to this: bloodstar & molecular
burning kiss. Conception. The grooved sockets slip into
each other, sinking into pain, a little deeper into earth's
habit. Tongue in juice meat, uncertain conversion, cock
& heart entangled, ragweed in bloom. A single sigh of
glory, the two put an armlock on each other—matched
for strength, leg over leg. Double bind & slow dance on
ball-bearing feet. Arm in arm & slipknot. Birth, death,
back to back—silent mouth against the other's ear. They
sing a duet: *e pluribus unum*. The spirit hinged to a
single tree. No deeper color stolen from midnight sky—
they're in the same shape, as meat collects around a
bone, almost immortal, like a centaur's future perfect
dream.

Books by Yusef Komunyakaa

Copacetic
I Apologize for the Eyes in My Head
Dedications & Other Dark Horses
Lost in the Bonewheel Factory
Toys in a Field

About the Author

Yusef Komunyakaa was born in Bogalusa, Louisiana; from 1984 to 1985 he was poet-in-the-schools in New Orleans, teaching students in the third through sixth grades. He is associate professor of English and was a visiting writer at Indiana University in 1985–86. He received a B.A. from the University of Colorado (1975), an M.A. from Colorado State University (1979), and an M.F.A. from the University of California at Irvine (1980). Komunyakaa's first book, *Copacetic,* was published by Wesleyan in 1984. He is the author also of several chapbooks.

About the Book

This book was typeset by G&S Typesetters, Inc. of Austin, Texas, in Galliard with Galliard display type, was printed on 60-pound Warren's Olde Style paper by Edwards Brothers, Inc., of Lillington, North Carolina, and was bound by Arcata Kingsport. The design is by Joyce Kachergis Book Design and Production of Bynum, North Carolina.

Wesleyan University Press, 1986